Keto Diet Lo
For Women Over 50

Simply And Tasty Recipes To Weight Loss And Healthy Eating Every Day

Emma Wilson

Table of Contents

LUNCH 47

DINNER 65

DESSERTS 83

INTRODUCTION

The ketogenic diet is a perfect combination of an equal number of macros essential for the human body's perfect and healthy functioning.

This diet is mostly focused on foods that are rich in fats, while carbohydrates are considerably lowered.

If you hadn't heard about the keto diet, you probably did not know that eating meals without balanced (or reduced) macros (carbohydrates, proteins, fats, and fibers) will lead to weight and fat.

When you provide your body with foods containing large amounts of carbohydrates (and fats and protein), your body stimulates insulin development, leading to leptin resistance. Slowly but surely, your body weight will increase. Not every organism is the same, but providing the body with unhealthy amounts of carbs combined with fats and proteins (without any physical activity) is a surefire way to end up obese.

How Keto Works

We will focus on how this diet works and how your body transitions from one way of functioning to another.

The ketogenic diet was used mainly to lower the incidence of seizures in epileptic children.

People wanted to check out how the keto diet would work with an entirely healthy person as things usually go.

This diet makes the body burn fats much faster than it does carbohydrates. The carbohydrates that we take in through food are turned into glucose, one of the leading "brain foods." So, once you start following the keto diet, food with reduced carbohydrates is forcing the liver to turn all the fats into fatty acids and ketone bodies. The ketones go to the brain and take the place of glucose, becoming the primary energy source. This is how your body turns towards the next best energy source to function correctly.

This diet's primary purpose is to make your body switch from the way it used to function to an entirely new way of creating energy, keeping you healthy and alive.

Once you start following the ketogenic diet, you will notice that things are changing, first and foremost, in your mind. Before, carbohydrates were your main body 'fuel' and were used to create glucose so that your brain could function. Now you no longer feed yourself with them.

In the beginning, most people feel odd because their natural food is off the table. When your menu consists of more fats and proteins, it is natural to feel that something is missing.

Your brain alarms you that you haven't eaten enough and sends you signals that you are hungry. It is literally "panicking" and telling you that you are starving, which is not correct. You get to eat, and you get to eat plenty of good food, but not carbs.

This condition usually arises during the first day or two. Afterward, people get used to their new eating habits.

Once the brain "realizes" that carbs are no longer an option, it will focus on "finding" another abundant energy source: in this case, fats.

Not only is your food rich in fats, but your body contains stored fats in large amounts. As you consume more fats and fewer carbs, your body "runs" on the fats, both consumed and stored. The best thing is that, as the fats are used for energy, they are burned. This is how you get a double gain from this diet.

Usually, it will take a few days of consuming low-carb meals before you start seeing visible weight loss results. You will not even have to check your weight because the fat layers will be visibly reduced.

This diet requires you to lower your daily consumption of carbs to only 20 grams. For most people, this transition from a regular carb-rich diet can be quite a challenge. Most people are used to eating bread, pasta, rice, dairy products, sweets, soda, alcohol, and fruits, so quitting all these foods might be challenging.

However, this is all in your head. If you manage to win the "battle" with your mind and endure the diet for a few days, you will see that you no longer have cravings as time goes by. Plus, the weight loss and the fat burn will be a great motivation to continue with this diet.

The keto diet practically makes the body burn fats much faster than carbohydrates; the foods you consume with this diet are quite rich in fats. Carbs will be there, too, but at far lower levels than before. Foods rich in carbohydrates are the body's primary fuel or the brain's food. (Our bodies turn carbs into glucose.) Because there are hardly any carbohydrates in this diet, the body will have to find a substitute source of energy to keep itself alive.

Many people who don't truly need to lose weight and are completely healthy still choose to follow the keto diet because it is a great way to keep their meals balanced. Also, it is the perfect way to cleanse the body of toxins, processed foods, sugars, and unnecessary carbs. The combination of these things is usually the main reason for heart failure, some cancers, diabetes, cholesterol, or obesity.

If you ask a nutritionist about this diet, they will recommend it without a doubt. So, if you feel like cleansing your body and starting a diet that will keep you healthy, well-fed, and slender, perhaps the keto diet should be your primary choice.

And what is the best thing about it (besides the fact that you will balance your weight and lower the risk of many diseases)?

There is no yo-yo effect. The keto diet can be followed forever and has no side effects. It does not restrict you from following it for a few weeks or a month. Once you get your body to keto foods, you will not think about going back to the old ways of eating your meals.

Benefits of the Keto Diet for Women over 50

When the entire ketogenic lifestyle is followed along with dietary changes, it results in the following known benefits:

1. Accelerates Metabolism

As a person ages, it is the rate of metabolism that slows down with time. Metabolism is the sum total of all the processes that are carried out in the body. It consists of the building of new cells and elements, as well as the breaking of the existing agents into other elements. The fat-sourced high energy and release of ketones accelerate the rate of metabolism in the body.

2. Hormones Production

It is said that a woman's body is particularly more sensitive to dietary changes than the male body. It is mainly because there are several hormones that are at play in a woman's body. With a slight change in dietary habits and lifestyle, women can harness more benefits out of their fasting regime. Hormones in women's bodies are not only responsible for regulating the mood and internal body processes, but they also affect other systems in the body. Controlled release of energy and a healthy diet is responsible for maintaining the balance of estrogen and progesterone in the body.

3. PCOS

Polycystic ovarian syndrome is another common disorder that is prevalent among women of all ages, especially those over 50. PCOS cases are often the result of consistently high levels of insulin in the blood. Therefore, the ketogenic diet, due to its lowering of insulin effect, can treat or prevent PCOS to some extent. It can also control and counter the negative effects of PCOS in women.

4. Diabetes

Insulin resistance is a condition in which the body resists producing insulin. When the body fails to produce insulin, the pancreatic cells produce more insulin to lower the blood glucose levels. Excessive insulin production over a longer period of time ultimately wears out the pancreatic cells, and they lose the ability to produce necessary insulin levels, thus leading to diabetes. Since intermittent fasting can prevent insulin resistance by naturally lowering blood glucose levels, it also reduces the risks of diabetes. The ketogenic diet controls the insulin levels in the blood, thus prevents the risks of insulin resistance and diabetes.

5. Oxidative Stress

There are various chemical reactions that are occurring within the human body as a result of metabolism. These reactions produce millions of products and byproducts. Some chemical reactions produce free radicals, which are highly reactive in nature. When these radicals are left in the body for a longer duration of time, they can oxidize other elements in the cells and mingle with the natural cell cycle, ultimately leading to cell death. The cumulative effect of those free radicals is termed oxidative stress. When this stress increases, it can negatively affect human health. Ketones produced through ketosis work as antioxidants, which remove the free radicals and toxins from the body.

6. Cures Cancer

The ketogenic diet also improves the immune system, which helps patients to fight against all sorts of diseases, especially cancer. When the body undergoes ketosis, there is an increased production of lymphocytes that kills the pathogens or agents that may lead to cancer. Several cancer treatments also use this natural immune system to fight against cancerous cells.

7. Inflammation

Inflammation is the swelling of body tissues and organs for any practical reason. In women over the age of 50, inflammation can result from hormonal or electrolyte imbalance. Accumulation of uric acid and high sugar and cholesterol levels may also cause inflammation. Diseases like osteoporosis, or arthritis, which are common among women, also cause inflammation. Similarly, inflammation can also occur in the brain due to Alzheimer's or dementia. In any case, inflammation is always painful and health-damaging. Ketosis can help the body fight against the agents, causing inflammation. It promotes the immune system to increase its productivity. The damaged cells, which cause inflammation in the neighboring area, are then actively removed through autophagy to clean the body and repair it.

8. Weight Loss

Finally, weight loss is the most promising and obvious advantage of the ketogenic diet. Women over 50 years of age actively seek the keto diet to lose weight. It can reduce two to three pounds of weight within a week.

BREAKFAST

Creamy Cinnamon Smoothie

Preparation Time: 5 minutes
Cooking Time: 0 minute
Servings: 2

Ingredients: 2 cups of coconut milk - 1 scoop vanilla protein powder - 5 drops liquid stevia - 1 teaspoon ground cinnamon - ½ teaspoon alcohol-free vanilla extract

Directions: Put the coconut milk, protein powder, stevia, cinnamon, and vanilla in a blender and blend until smooth. Pour into 2 glasses and serve immediately.

Nutrition: Calories: 492 cal / Fat: 47g / Carbs: 8g / Protein: 18g / Fiber: 2g

Keto Mushroom Sausage Skillet

Preparation Time: 5 minutes

Cooking Time: 25 minutes

Servings: 5

Ingredients:

Sixteen ounces of cremini mushroom

Sixteen ounces of pork sausage

One cup of mozzarella cheese, grated

Two tablespoons of olive oil

Two medium green onions, for garnish

Directions:

Collect all ingredients and cook them. To heat it, switch on the oven to broil. Load half the olive oil onto a cast iron skillet and switch on medium heat on the stovetop. Wash the mushrooms, dry them well with a paper towel, and cut them into strips. Cook the sausages in the cast iron skillet on the stovetop over medium to high heat until they are golden and thoroughly fried. Remove the sausages from the pan until they are thoroughly cooked and arrange them on a cutting board. Add the remaining olive oil to the skillet, add the mushrooms and cook until the mushrooms are golden brown. Chop up the pork sausage on a cutting board while the mushrooms are frying, with a diagonal break. Add the sliced pork sausage to the skillet and scatter with mozzarella cheese as soon as the mushrooms are thoroughly cooked. Place it on a grill inside the oven until the cheese begins to melt. Look closely at the microwave. The cheese melts quickly! Remove and garnish with green onions from the oven.

Nutrition:

Calories 357

Fat 25g

Carbohydrates 4.5g

Protein 22g

Creamy Almond and Cheese Mix

Preparation Time: 10 minutes
Cooking Time: 20 minutes
Servings: 6

Ingredients: 1-cup almond milk - Cooking spray - 9 ounces cream cheese, soft - 1 cup cheddar cheese, shredded - 6 spring onions, chopped - Salt and black pepper to the taste - 6 eggs, whisked

Directions: Heat up your air fryer with the oil at 350 degrees F and grease it with cooking spray. In a bowl, put and mixed the eggs with the rest of the ingredients, whisk well, pour and spread into the air fryer and cook everything for 20 minutes. Divide everything between plates and serve.

Nutrition: Calories 231 / Fat 11g / Fiber 3g / Carbohydrates 5g / Protein 8g

Eggs and Cheddar Breakfast Burritos

Preparation Time: 15 minutes
Cooking Time: 6 minutes
Servings: 4

Ingredients: 3 tbsp butter - 2 small yellow onions, chopped ½ medium orange bell pepper, deseeded and chopped - 10 eggs, beaten - Salt and black pepper to taste - 8 tbsp grated cheddar cheese (white and sharp) - 4 (8-inch) low-carb soft tortillas - 2 tbsp chopped fresh scallions. Hot sauce for serving

Directions: Melt the butter in a skillet over medium heat and stir-fry the onions and bell pepper for 3 minutes or until softened. Pour the eggs into the pan, let set for 15 seconds and then, scramble. Season with salt, black pepper, and stir in the cheddar cheese. Cook until the cheese melts. Lay out the tortillas, divide the eggs on top, and sprinkle some scallions and hot sauce on top. Fold two edges of each tortilla in and tightly roll the other ends over the filling. Slice into halves and enjoy the burritos.

Nutrition: Calories: 478 Cal / Fat: 27 g / Carbs: 7 g / Protein: 14 g / Fiber: 5 g

Ricotta Omelet with Swiss Chard

Preparation Time: 10 minutes
Cooking Time: 15 minutes
Servings: 2

Ingredients: 6 eggs - 2 tbsp. almond milk - ½ tsp. kosher salt ½ tsp. ground black pepper - 6 tbsp. unsalted butter, divided 2 bunch Swiss chard, cleaned and stemmed - 2/3 cup ricotta

Directions: Add the eggs, and milk. Season with salt and pepper then whisk. Set aside. In a skillet, melt 4 tbsp. butter. Add the veggie leaves and sauté until just wilted. Remove from pan. Set aside. Now melt 1 tbsp. butter in the skillet. Add half of the egg mixture. Spread the mixture. Cook for about 2 minutes. Add half of the ricotta when the edges are firm, but the center is still a bit runny. Bend 1/3 of the omelet over the ricotta filling. Transfer to a plate. Repeat with the remaining butter and egg mixture. Serve with Swiss chard.

Nutrition: Calories: 693 / Fat: 60g / Carb: 8g / Protein: 2g

Omelet with Goat Cheese and Herb

Preparation Time: 5 minutes
Cooking Time: 12 minutes
Servings: 2

Ingredients: 6 eggs, beaten - 2 tbsp. chopped herbs (basil, parsley or cilantro) - Kosher salt and black pepper to taste - 2 tbsp. unsalted butter - 4 ounces fresh goat cheese

Directions: Whisk together the eggs, herbs, salt, and pepper. Melt 1 tbsp. butter in a skillet. Put half of the egg mixture and cook for 4 to 5 minutes, or until just set. Crumble half the goatcheese over the eggs and fold in half. Cook for 1 minute, or until cheese is melted. Transfer to a plate. Repeat process with the remaining butter, egg mixture, and goat cheese. Serve.

Nutrition: Calories: 523 / Fat: 43g / Carb: 3g / Protein: 31g

Bacon and Zucchini Egg Breakfast

Preparation Time: 10 minutes
Cooking Time: 10 minutes
Servings: 2

Ingredients:

2 cups zucchini noodles

2 slices of raw bacon

¼ cup grated Asiago cheese

2 eggs - Salt and pepper to taste

Directions : Cut the bacon slices into ¼ inch thick strips. Cook the bacon in a pan for 3 minutes. Add the zucchini and mix well. Season with salt and pepper. Flatten slightly with a spatula and make 2 depressions for the eggs. Sprinkle with the cheese. Break one egg into each dent. Cook 3 minutes more, then cover and cook for 2 to 4 minutes, or until the eggs are cooked. Serve.

Nutrition: Calories: 242 / Fat: 19g / Carb: 4g / Protein: 14g

Chia Breakfast Bowl

Preparation Time: 10 minutes

Cooking Time: 0 minutes

Servings: 2

Ingredients:

¼ cup whole chia seeds

2 cups almond milk, unsweetened

2 tbsp. sugar-free maple syrup

1 tsp. vanilla extract.

Toppings: Cinnamon and extra maple syrup - Nuts and berries

Directions: Combine the syrup, milk, chia seeds, and vanilla extract in a bowl and stir to mix. Let stand for 30 minutes, then whisk. Transfer to an airtight container. Cover and refrigerate overnight. Serve in the morning.

Nutrition: Calories: 298 / Fat: 15g / Carb: 5g / Protein: 14g

Bacon Omelet

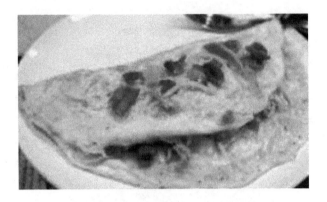

Preparation Time: 10 minutes
Cooking Time: 15 minutes
Servings: 3

Ingredients:

4 large organic eggs

1 tablespoon fresh chives, minced

Salt and ground black pepper, as required

4 bacon slices

1 tablespoon unsalted butter

2 ounces cheddar cheese, shredded

Directions:

In a bowl, add the eggs, chives, salt, and black pepper, and beat until well combined. Heat a non-stick frying pan over medium-high heat and cook the bacon slices for about 8–10 minutes. Place the bacon onto a paper towel-lined plate to drain. Then chop the bacon slices. With paper towels, wipe out the frying pan. In the same frying pan, melt butter over medium-low heat and cook the egg mixture for about 2 minutes. Carefully, flip the omelet and top with chopped bacon. Cook for 1–2 minutes or until desired doneness of eggs. Remove from heat and immediately, place the cheese in the center of omelet. Fold the edges of omelet over cheese and cut into 2 portions. Serve immediately.

Nutrition:

Calories 427

Total Carbs 1.2g

Fiber 0g

Sugar 1g

Protein 29.1g

Bacon & Avocado Omelet

Preparation Time: 5 minutes
Cooking Time: 5 minutes
Servings: 1

Ingredients: 1 slice Crispy bacon - 2 Large organic eggs - 5 cup freshly grated parmesan cheese - 2 tbsp Ghee or coconut oil or butter - half of 1 small Avocado

Directions: Prepare the bacon to your liking and set aside. Combine the eggs, parmesan cheese, and your choice of finely chopped herbs. Warm a skillet and add the butter/ghee to melt using the medium-high heat setting. When the pan is hot, whisk and add the eggs. Prepare the omelet working it towards the middle of the pan for about 30 seconds. When firm, flip, and cook it for another 30 seconds. Arrange the omelet on a plate and garnish with the crunched bacon bits. Serve with sliced avocado.

Nutrition: Carbs: 3.3 g / Protein: 30 g / Fats: 63 g / Calories: 719

Bagels With Cheese

Preparation Time: 10 minutes
Cooking Time: 15 minutes
Servings: 6

Ingredients:

2.5 cups Mozzarella cheese

1 tsp. Baking powder

3 oz Cream cheese

1.5 cups Almond flour - 2 Eggs

Directions: Shred the mozzarella and combine with the flour, baking powder, and cream cheese in a mixing container. Pop into the microwave for about one minute. Mix well. Let the mixture cool and add the eggs. Break apart into six sections and shape into round bagels. Note: You can also sprinkle with a seasoning of your choice or pinch of salt if desired. Bake them for approximately 12 to 15 minutes. Serve or cool and store.

Nutrition: Carbs: 8 g / Protein: 19 g / Fats: 31 g / Calories: 374

Baked Apples

Preparation Time: 10 minutes
Cooking Time: 1 hour
Servings: 4

Ingredients:

4 tsp Keto-friendly sweetener

75 tsp Cinnamon

25 cup chopped pecans

4 large Granny Smith apples

Directions: Set the oven temperature at 375° Fahrenheit. Mix the sweetener with the cinnamon and pecans. Core the apple and add the prepared stuffing. Add enough water into the baking dish to cover the bottom of the apple. Bake them for about 45 minutes to 1 hour.

Nutrition: Carbs: 16 g / Protein: 6.8 g / Fats: 19.9 g / Calories: 175

Baked Eggs In The Avocado

Preparation Time: 10 minutes

Cooking Time: 20 minutes

Servings: 1

Ingredients:

half of 1 Avocado

1 Egg

1 tbsp Olive oil

Half cup shredded cheddar cheese

Directions: Heat the oven to reach 425° Fahrenheit. Discard the avocado pit and remove just enough of the 'insides' to add the egg. Drizzle with oil and break the egg into the shell. Sprinkle with cheese and bake them for 15 to 16 minutes until the egg is the way you prefer. Serve.

Nutrition: Carbs: 3 g / Protein: 21 g / Fats: 52 g / Calories: 452

SNACKS , SIDES AND APPETIZERS

Coconut Cauliflower Mash

Preparation Time: 10 minutes
Cooking Time: 10 minutes
Servings: 6

Ingredients: 2 cauliflower heads, florets separated - 1/3 cup coconut cream - 1/3 cup coconut milk - 1 tablespoon chives, chopped - A pinch of salt and black pepper

Directions: Put some water in a pot, bring to a boil over medium-high heat, add cauliflower florets, cook them for 10 minutes, drain them well, mash using a potato masher and stir. Add the cream, the coconut milk, salt, pepper and chives, stir well, divide between plates and serve as a side dish.

Nutrition: Calories: 200 / Fat: 3g / Fiber: 3g / Carbohydrates: 12g Protein: 5g

Parmesan Brussels Sprouts

Preparation Time: 10 minutes
Cooking Time: 30 minutes
Servings: 4

Ingredients: 1-pound Brussels sprouts, halved - 1 teaspoon oregano, dried -1 tablespoon olive oil - 3 garlic cloves, minced - ½ teaspoon hot paprika - A pinch of salt and black pepper - 2 tablespoons keto ranch dressing - 1 tablespoon parmesan, grated

Directions: Spread the sprouts on a lined baking sheet, add oregano, oil, garlic, paprika, salt and pepper, toss, bake them in the oven at 425 degrees F for 30 minutes, add parmesan and keto ranch dressing, toss well, divide between plates and serve as a side dish.

Nutrition: Calories: 222 / Fat: 4g / Fiber: 6g / Carbohydrates: 12g Protein: 8g

Fried Cauliflower Rice

Preparation Time: 10 minutes
Cooking Time: 15 minutes
Servings: 4

Ingredients: 1 tablespoon ghee, melted - 1 small yellow onion, chopped - 2 hot dogs, sliced - 1 tablespoon avocado oil - 1 garlic clove, minced - 2 and ½ cups cauliflower rice, steamed - 2 eggs, whisked - 2 tablespoons coconut amino - 2 scallions, sliced

Directions: Heat up a pan with the ghee over medium-high heat, add onion, garlic and hot dogs, stir and cook for 5 minutes. Add cauliflower rice and avocado oil, stir and cook for 5 minutes more. Add the eggs, toss everything, cook for 5 more minutes until the eggs are scrambled, add the amino and the scallions, toss, divide between plates and serve as a side dish.

Nutrition: Calories: 200 / Fat: 3g / Fiber: 6g / Carbohydrates: 12g Protein: 8g

Preparation Time: 10 minutes
Cooking Time: 30 minutes
Servings: 6

Ingredients:

3 garlic cloves, minced

¾ cup coconut cream

2 pounds asparagus, trimmed

1 cup parmesan, grated

A pinch of salt and black pepper

1 cup mozzarella, shredded

Directions: In a baking dish, combine the asparagus with the garlic, cream, salt, pepper, mozzarella and top with the parmesan, introduce in the oven and bake at 400 degrees F for 30 minutes. Divide between plates and serve as a side dish.

Nutrition: Calories: 200 / Fat: 3g / Fiber: 6g / Carbohydrates: 12g Protein: 9g

Crunchy Parmesan Crisps

Preparation Time: 5 minutes
Cooking Time: 3 minutes
Servings: 12

Ingredients:

12 tablespoons Parmesan cheese, shredded

Directions: Preheat your oven to 400° Fahrenheit. Spray a baking tray with cooking spray. Place each tablespoon of cheese on a baking tray. Bake in preheated oven for 3 minutes or until lightly brown. Allow cooling time, serve, and enjoy!

Nutrition:

Calories: 64 / Carbohydrates: 0.7 g

Sugar: 0 g / Fat: 4.3 g

Cholesterol: 14 mg / Protein: 6.4 g

Roasted Cauliflower with Prosciutto, Capers, and Almonds.

Preparation Time: 10 minutes
Cooking Time: 25 minutes
Servings: 2

Ingredients:

12 ounces cauliflower florets (I get precut florets at Trader Joe's)

2 tablespoons leftover bacon grease, or olive oil

Pink Himalayan salt - Freshly ground black pepper

2 ounces sliced prosciutto, torn into small pieces

¼ cup slivered almonds - 2 tablespoons capers

2 tablespoons grated Parmesan cheese

Directions:

Preheat the oven to 400 degrees F. Line a baking pan with a silicone baking mat or parchment paper. Put the cauliflower florets in the prepared baking pan with the bacon grease, and season with pink Himalayan salt and pepper. Or if you are using olive oil instead, drizzle the cauliflower with olive oil and season with pink Himalayan salt and pepper. Roast the cauliflowerfor 15 minutes. Stir the cauliflower so all sides are coated with the bacon grease. Distribute the prosciutto pieces in the pan. Then add the slivered almonds and capers. Stir to combine. Sprinkle the Parmesan cheese on top, and roast for 10 minutes more. Divide between two plates, using a slotted spoon so you don't get excess grease in the plates, and serve.

Nutrition:

Calories: 288

Fat: 24g

Carbohydrates: 7g

Fiber: 3g

Protein: 14g

Chipotle Jicama Hash

Preparation Time: 5 minutes
Cooking Time: 10 minutes
Servings: 5

Ingredients: 4 slices bacon, chopped - 12 oz. jicama, peeled and diced - 4 oz. purple onion, chopped - 1 oz. green bell pepper (or poblano), seeded and chopped - 4 tbsp. Chipotle mayonnaise

Directions: Using a skillet, brown the bacon on a high heat. Remove and place on a towel to drain the grease. Use the remaining grease to fry the onions and jicama until brown. When ready, add the bell pepper and cook the hash until tender. Transfer the hash onto two plates and serve each plate with 4 tablespoons of Chipotle mayonnaise.

Nutrition: Calories 175 kcal/Protein 5.39 g/Fat 13.29 g/Carbs 8.79 g

Fried Queso Blanco

Preparation Time: 20 minutes + 2 hours freezing time

Cooking Time: 30 minutes

Servings: 4

Ingredients: 5 oz. queso Blanco - 1 ½ tbsp. olive oil - 3 oz. cheese 2 oz. olives- 1 pinch red pepper flakes

Directions: Cube some cheese and freeze it for 1-2 hours. Pour the oil in a skillet and heat to boil over a medium temperature. Add the cheese cubes and heat till brown. Combine the cheese together using a spatula and flatten.cook the cheese on both sides, flipping regularly. While flipping, fold the cheese into itself to form crispy layers. Use a spatula to roll it into a block. Remove it from the pan, allow it to cool, cut it into small cubes, and serve.

Nutrition: Calories: 282 kcal / Protein: 12.55 g / Fat: 23.94 g Carbohydrates: 4.87 g

Spinach with Bacon & Shallots

Preparation Time: 5 minutes
Cooking Time: 25 minutes
Servings: 4

Ingredients: 16 oz. raw spinach - ½ cup chopped white onion ½ cup chopped shallot - ½ pound raw bacon slices - 2 tbsp. butter

Directions: Slice the bacon strips into small narrow pieces. In a skillet, heat the butter and add the chopped onion, shallots, and bacon. Sauté for 15-20 minutes or until the onions start to caramelize, and the bacon is cooked. Add the spinach and sauté on medium heat. Stir frequently to ensure the leaves touch the skillet while cooking. Cover and steam for around 5 minutes, stir and continue until wilted. Serve!

Nutrition: Calories: 361 kcal / Protein: 12.59 g / Fat: 31.04 g Carbohydrates: 10.1 g

Bacon-Wrapped Sausage Skewers

Preparation Time: 10 minutes
Cooking Time: 8 minutes
Servings: 4

Ingredients:

5 Italian chicken sausages

10 slices bacon

Directions: Preheat your deep fryer to 370°F/190°C. Cut the sausage into four pieces. Slice the bacon in half. Wrap the bacon over the sausage. Skewer the sausage. Fry for 4-5 minutes until browned.

Nutrition:

Calories: 331 kcal

Protein: 11.84 g

Fat: 30.92 g

Carbohydrates: 1.06 g

Brussels Sprout Chips

Preparation Time: 6 minutes
Cooking Time: 20 minutes
Servings: 4

Ingredients: 1 teaspoon garlic powder - 1/2 lb. brussels sprouts, sliced thinly - 1 tablespoon extra-virgin olive oil - 2 tablespoons Parmesan, grated - Kosher salt and black pepper, to taste

Directions: At 400 degrees F, preheat your oven. Toss brussels sprouts with parmesan, garlic powder, oil, black pepper, and salt. Spread the brussels sprouts in the baking sheet in a single layer. Bake them for 10 minutes in the preheated oven. Toss them well, then bake again for 10 minutes until crispy. Serve warm and crispy.

Nutrition: Calories 102 / Total Fat 6.7g / Saturated Fat 2.6g Cholesterol 10mg / Sodium 144mg / Total Carbohydrate 6.2g / Dietary Fiber 2.2g / Total Sugars 1.4g / Protein 6.6g

Spicy Roasted Pecans

Preparation Time: 5 minutes
Cooking Time: 10 minutes
Servings: 9

Ingredients:

1 teaspoon salt

8 oz. pecans

1 tablespoon coconut oil

1 teaspoon paprika powder

Directions: At 325 degrees F, preheat your oven. Toss pecans with salt, coconut oil, and paprika powder in a suitable bowl. Spread the pecan in a baking sheet. Roast the spicy pecans for 10 minutes in the preheated oven. Toss the pecans when cooked halfway through. Serve and enjoy.

Nutrition: Calories 189 / Total Fat 19.6g / Saturated Fat 2g Cholesterol 0mg / Sodium 260mg / Total Carbohydrate 3.6g / Dietary Fiber 2.7g / Total Sugars 0.9g / Protein 2.7g

LUNCH

Turkey Breast with Tomato-Olive Salsa

Preparation Time: 20 minutes
Cooking Time: 10 minutes
Servings: 4

Ingredients:

For turkey: 4 boneless turkey. Skinned - 3 tablespoons olive oil - Salt -Pepper

For salsa: 6 chopped tomatoes - 1/2 diced onions - 5 ounces of pitted and chopped olives - 2 crushed garlic cloves - 2 tablespoons of chopped basil - 1 large diced jalapeno - Pepper - Salt

Directions: In a bowl, put salt, pepper, and three spoons of oil, mix and coat the turkey with this mixture. Place it on a preheated grill and grill for ten minutes. In another bowl, mix garlic, olives, tomatoes, pepper, and drop the rest of the oil. Sprinkle salt and toss. Serve this salsa with turkey is warm.

Nutrition: Calories: 387 / Fat: 12.5g / Fiber: 8.4g / Carbs: 3.1 g Protein: 18.6g

Turkey Meatballs

Preparation Time: 15 minutes
Cooking Time: 20 minutes
Servings: 2

Ingredients: 1 pound of ground turkey - 1 tablespoon of fish sauce 1 diced onion - 2 tablespoons of soy sauce - 1/2 almond flour - 1/8 cup of ground beef - 1/2 teaspoon of garlic powder - 1/2 teaspoon of salt 1/2 teaspoon of ground ginger - 1/2 teaspoon of thyme - 1/2 teaspoon of curry - 5 tablespoons of olive oil

Directions: Combine ground turkey, fish sauce, one diced onion, soy sauce, ground beef, seasonings, oil, and flour in a large mixing bowl. Mix it thoroughly. Form meatballs depending on preferred size. Heat skillet and pour in 3 tablespoons of oil [you may need more depending on the size of meat balls]. Cook meatballs until evenly browned on each side. Serve hot.

Nutrition: Calories: 281 / Fat: 11.6g / Fiber: 6.9g / Carbs:4.6 g Protein: 15.1g

Cheesy Bacon Ranch Chicken

Preparation Time: 40 minutes
Cooking Time: 35 minutes
Servings: 8

Ingredients: 8 boneless and skinned chicken breasts - 1 cup of olive oil - 8 thick slices bacon 3 cups of shredded mozzarella - 1 1/4 tablespoon of ranch seasoning - 1 small chopped onion - Chopped chives - Kosher salt or pink salt - Black pepper

Directions: Preheat skillet and heat little oil, and cook bacon evenly on both sides. Save four tablespoons of drippings and put the others away. Add in salt and pepper in a bowl and rub it over chicken to season. Put 1/2 oil on the flame to cook the chicken from each side for 5 to 7 minutes. When ready, reduce the heat and put in the ranch seasoning, then add mozzarella. Cover and cook on a low flame for 3-5 minutes.Put in bacon fat and chopped chives, then bacon and cover it. Take off and serve warm.

Nutrition: Calories: 387 / Fat: 15.1g / Fiber: 10.6g / Carbs:5.9 g Protein: 12.9g

Beef & Veggie Casserole

Preparation Time: 20 minutes
Cooking Time: 55 minutes
Servings: 4

Ingredients: 3tbsp butter - 1-pound grass-fed ground beef - 1 yellow onion - 2 garlic cloves 1cup pumpkin - 1cup broccoli - 2cups cheddar cheese - 1tbsp Dijon mustard - 6 organic eggs ½cup heavy whipping cream - Salt - ground black pepper

Directions: Cook the beef within 8–10 minutes. Transfer. Cook the onion and garlic within 10 minutes. Add the pumpkin and cook within 5–6 minutes. Add the broccoli and cook within 3–4 minutes. Transfer to the cooked beef, combine. Warm-up oven to 350°F. Put 2/3 of cheese and mustard in the beef mixture, combine. In another mixing bowl, add cream, eggs, salt, and black pepper, and beat. In a baking dish, place the beef mixture and top with egg mixture, plus the remaining cheese. Bake within 25 minutes. Serve.

Nutrition: Calories 472 / Carbs 5.5 g / Fat 34.6 g / Sodium 463 mg Protein 32.6 g

---

Beef with Bell Peppers

Preparation Time: 15 minutes

Cooking Time: 10 minutes

Servings: 6

Ingredients: 1tbsp olive oil - 1-pound grass-fed flank steak - 1 red bell pepper - 1 green bell pepper - 1tbsp ginger - 3tbsp low-sodium soy sauce - 1½tbsp balsamic vinegar - 2tsp Sriracha

Directions: Sear the steak slices within 2 minutes. Cook bell peppers within 2–3 minutes. Transfer the beef mixture. Boil the remaining fixing within 1 minute. Add the beef mixture and cook within 1–2 minutes. Serve.

Nutrition: Calories 274 / Carbs 3.8 g / Fat 13.1 g / Protein 32.9 g

Braised Lamb shanks

Preparation Time: 15 minutes
Cooking Time: 2 hours 35 minutes
Servings: 6

Ingredients: 4 grass-fed lamb shanks - 2tbsp butter - Salt - ground black pepper - 6 garlic cloves - 6 rosemary sprigs - 1cup chicken broth

Directions: Warm-up oven to 450°F. Coat the shanks with butter and put salt plus pepper. Roast within 20 minutes. Remove then reduce to 325°F. Place the garlic cloves and rosemary over and around the lamb. Roast within 2 hours. Put the broth into a roasting pan. Increase to 400°F. Roast within 15 minutes more. Serve.

Nutrition: Calories 1093 / Carbs 2 g / Fat 44.2 g / Protein 161.4 g

Shrimp & Bell Pepper Stir-Fry

Preparation Time: 20 minutes
Cooking Time: 10 minutes
Servings: 3

Ingredients: ½cup low-sodium soy sauce - 2tablespoons balsamic vinegar - 2tablespoons Erythritol - 1tablespoon arrowroot starch 1tablespoon ginger - ½teaspoon red pepper flakes - 3tablespoons olive oil - ½ red bell pepper - ½ yellow bell pepper - ½ green bell pepper - 1 onion - 1 red chili - 1½ pounds shrimp - 2 scallion greens

Directions: Mix soy sauce, vinegar, erythritol, arrowroot starch, ginger, and red pepper flakes. Set aside. Stir-fry the bell peppers, onion, and red chili within 1–2 minutes. In the center of the wok, place the shrimp and cook within 1–2 minutes. Stir the shrimp with bell pepper mixture and cook within 2 minutes. Stir in the sauce and cook within 2–3 minutes. Stir in the scallion greens and remove. Serve hot.

Nutrition: Calories 221 / Carbs 6.5 g / Fat 9 g / Protein 27.6 g

Salad Skewers

Preparation time: 10 minutes
Cooking time: 0 minute
Servings: 1

Ingredients:

- Two wooden skewers, soaked in water for 30 min. before use
- Eight large black olives
- Eight cherry tomatoes
- One yellow pepper, cut into eight squares
- ½ red onion, chopped in half and separated into eight pieces
- 3.5-ounce (about 10cm) cucumber, cut into four slices and halved ounce of feta, cut into eight cubes
- For the dressing:
- 1 tablespoon extra virgin olive oil
- 1 teaspoon balsamic vinegar
- Juice of ½ lemon
- Few leaves basil, finely chopped (or ½ tsp dried mixed herbs to replace basil and oregano)

- A right amount of salt and freshly ground black pepper
- Few leaves oregano, finely chopped
- ½ clove garlic, peeled and crushed

Directions:

Thread each skewer in the order with salad ingredients: olive, tomato, yellow pepper, red onion, cucumber, feta, basil, olive, yellow pepper, red ointment, cucumber, feta. Put all the ingredients of the dressing in a small bowl and blend well together. Pour over the spoils.

Nutrition:

Calories 315

Fat 30g

Protein 56g

Carbohydrate 45g

Cholesterol 230mg

Sugar 0g

Veggies & Walnut Loaf

Preparation Time: 15 minutes
Cooking Time: 1 hour 10 minutes
Servings: 3

Ingredients: 1 tablespoon olive oil - 2 yellow onions - 2 garlic cloves 1 teaspoon dried rosemary – 1 cup walnuts - 2 carrots - 1 celery stalk 1 green bell pepper – 1 cup button mushrooms - 5 organic eggs 1 ¼cups almond flour - Salt - ground black pepper

Directions: Warm-up oven to 350°F. Sauté the onion within 4–5 minutes. Add the garlic and rosemary and sauté within 1 minute. Add the walnuts and vegetables within 3–4 minutes. Put asideBeat the eggs, flour, sea salt, and black pepper.Mix the egg mixture with vegetable mixture. Bake within 50–60 minutes. Serve.

Nutrition: Calories 242 / Carbs 4.6 g / Fat 19.5 g / Protein 5.9 g

Rib Roast

Preparation Time: 15 minutes
Cooking Time: 3 hours
Servings: 6

Ingredients: 1 rib roast - Salt to taste - 12 cloves garlic, chopped 2 teaspoons lemon zest - 6 tablespoons fresh rosemary, chopped 5 sprigs thyme

Directions: Preheat your oven to 325 degrees F. Season all sides of rib roast with salt. Place the rib roast in a baking pan. Sprinkle with garlic, lemon zest and rosemary. Add herb sprigs on top. Roast for 3 hours. Let rest for a few minutes and then slice and serve.

Nutrition: Calories 329 / Total Fat 27g / Saturated Fat 9g Cholesterol 59mg / Sodium 498mg / Total Carbohydrate 5.3g Dietary Fiber 1.8g / Protein 18g / Total Sugars 2g / Potassium 493mg

Beef Stir Fry

Preparation Time: 15 minutes
Cooking Time: 10 minutes
Servings: 4

Ingredients: 1 tablespoon soy sauce - 1 tablespoon ginger, minced - 1 teaspoon cornstarch - 1 teaspoon dry sherry - 12 oz. beef, sliced into strips - 1 teaspoon toasted sesame oil - 2 tablespoons oyster sauce - 1 lb. baby bok choy, sliced - 3 tablespoons chicken broth

Directions: Mix soy sauce, ginger, cornstarch and dry sherry in a bowl. Toss the beef in the mixture. Pour oil into a pan over medium heat. Cook the beef for 5 minutes, stirring. Add oyster sauce, bok choy and chicken broth to the pan. Cook for 1 minute.

Nutrition: Calories 247 / Total Fat 15.8 g / Saturated Fat 4 g Cholesterol 69 mg / Sodium 569 mg / Total Carbohydrate 6.3 g Dietary Fiber 1.1 g / Protein 25 g

Sweet & Sour Pork

Preparation Time: 15 minutes
Cooking Time: 15 minutes
Servings: 6

Ingredients: 1 lb. pork chops - Salt and pepper to taste - ½ cup sesame seeds - 2 tablespoons peanut oil - 2 tablespoons soy sauce 3 tablespoons apricot jam - Chopped scallions

Directions: Season pork chops with salt and pepper. Press sesame seeds on both sides of pork. Pour oil into a pan over medium heat. Cook pork for 3 to 5 minutes per side. Transfer to a plate. In a bowl, mix soy sauce and apricot jam. Simmer for 3 minutes. Pour sauce over the pork and garnish with scallions before serving.

Nutrition: Calories 414 / Total Fat 27.5 g / Saturated Fat 5.6 g Cholesterol 68 mg / Sodium 607 mg / Total Carbohydrate 12.9 g Dietary Fiber 1.8 g / Protein 29 g / Sugars 9 g / Potassium 332 mg

Grilled Pork with Salsa

Preparation Time: 30 minutes
Cooking Time: 15 minutes
Servings: 8

Ingredients: Salsa - 1 onion, chopped - 1 tomato, chopped - 1 peach, chopped - 1 apricot, chopped - 1 tablespoon olive oil - 1 tablespoon lime juice - 2 tablespoons fresh cilantro, chopped - Salt and pepper to taste -Pork - 1 lb. pork tenderloin, sliced - 1 tablespoon olive oil - Salt and pepper to taste - ½ teaspoon ground cumin - ¾ teaspoon chili powder

Directions: Combine salsa ingredients in a bowl. Cover and refrigerate. Brush pork tenderloin with oil. Season with salt, pepper, cumin and chili powder. Grill pork for 5 to 7 minutes per side. Slice pork and serve with salsa.

Nutrition: Calories 219 / Total Fat 9.5 g / Saturated Fat 1.8 g Cholesterol 74 mg / Sodium 512 mg / Total Carbohydrate 8.3 g Dietary Fiber 1.5 g / Protein 24 g / Sugars 6 g / Potassium 600 mg

Garlic Pork Loin

Preparation Time: 15 minutes

Cooking Time: 1 hour

Servings: 6

Ingredients:

1 ½ lb. pork loin roast

4 cloves garlic, sliced into slivers

Salt and pepper to taste

Directions: Preheat your oven to 425 degrees F. Make several slits all over the pork roast. Insert garlic slivers. Sprinkle with salt and pepper. Roast in the oven for 1 hour.

Nutrition: Calories 235 / Total Fat 13.3 g / Total Carbohydrate 1.7 g / Dietary Fiber 0.3 g / Protein 25.7 g / Total Sugars 3 g

Keto Sloppy Joes

Preparation Time: 15 minutes
Cooking Time: 1 hour 10 minutes
Servings: 2

Ingredients:

1 ¼cup almond flour

5 tbsp. ground psyllium husk powder

1 tsp. sea salt - 2 tsp. baking powder

2 tsp. cider vinegar - 1 ¼ cups boiling water

3 egg whites – 2 tbsp. olive oil

1 ½ lb. ground beef - 1 yellow onion

4 garlic cloves – 14 oz. crushed tomatoes

1 tbsp. chili powder - 1 tbsp. Dijon powder

1 tbsp. red wine vinegar – 4 tbsp. tomato paste

2 tsp. salt - ¼ tsp ground black pepper

½ cup mayonnaise - 6 oz. cheese

Directions:

Warm-up the oven to 350 degrees and then mix all the dry fixing. Add some vinegar, egg whites, and boiled water. Whisk for 30 seconds. Form the dough into 5 or 8 pieces of bread. Cook within 55 minutes. Cook the onion and garlic. Add the ground beef and cook. Put the other fixing and cook. Simmer for 10 minutes in low. Serve.

Nutrition:

Calories: 215

Carbs: 19g

Fat: 10g

Protein: 30g

DINNER

Skillet Chicken with White Wine Sauce

Preparation Time: 5 minutes
Cooking Time: 30 minutes
Servings: 4

Ingredients: 4 boneless chicken thighs - 1 tsp. garlic powder - 1 tsp. dried thyme - 1 tbsp. olive oil - 1 tbsp. butter - 1 yellow onion diced 3 garlic cloves minced - 1 cup dry white wine - ½ cup heavy cream fresh chopped parsley - salt and pepper

Directions: Heat your oil in a skillet. Season your chicken, add it to the skillet, and then cook it about 5-7 mins. Flip the chicken and cook until looking golden brown. Remove the chicken to a plate. Add butter to the skillet. Then add onions and cook them until softened. Stir in garlic, salt and pepper, add the wine and cook for 4-5 mins. Stir in the thyme and the heavy cream. Place the breasts back to the skillet and leave to simmer for 2-3 mins. Top them with the parsley.

Nutrition: Calories 276 kcal / Fats 21 g / Carbs 6 g / Protein 25 g

Stir Fry Kimchi and Pork Belly

Preparation Time: 10 minutes
Cooking Time: 18 minutes
Servings: 3

Ingredients:

300 g pork belly

1 lb. kimchi

1 tbsp. soy sauce

1 tbsp. rice wine

1 tbsp. sesame seeds

1 stalk green onion

Directions: Slice the pork as thin as possible and marinate it in soy sauce and rice wine for 8-10 mins. Heat a pan. When very hot, add the pork belly and stir-fry until brown. Add the kimchi to the pan and stir-fry for 2 mins to let the flavors completely mix. Turn off heat and slice the green onion. Top with sesame seeds.

Nutrition: Calories 790 kcal / Fats 68 g / Carbs 7 g / Protein 14 g

Broccoli Soup

Preparation Time: 12 minutes
Cooking Time: 35 minutes
Servings: 4

Ingredients: 2 cloves garlic - 1 medium white onion - 1 tbsp butter - 2 cups of water - 2 cups vegetable stock - 1 cup heavy cream - Salt and ground black pepper to taste - ½ tsp paprika - 1½ cups broccoli, divided into florets - 1 cup cheddar cheese

Directions: Peel and mince garlic. Peel and chop the onion. Preheat pot on medium heat, add butter and melt it. Add garlic and onion and sauté for 5 minutes, stirring occasionally. Pour in water, vegetable stock, heavy cream, and add pepper, salt and paprika. Stir and bring to boil. Add broccoli and simmer for 25 minutes. After that, transfer soup mixture to a food processor and blend well. Grate cheddar cheese and add to a food processor, blend again. Serve soup hot.

Nutrition: Calories: 348 / Carbs: 6.8g / Fat: 33.8g / Protein: 10.9g

Simple Tomato Soup

Preparation Time: 15 minutes
Cooking Time: 10 minutes
Servings: 6

Ingredients: 4 cups canned tomato soup - 2 tbsp apple cider vinegar - 1 tsp dried oregano - 4 tbsp butter - 2 tsp turmeric - 2 oz red hot sauce - Salt and ground black pepper to taste - 4 tbsp olive oil - 8 bacon strips, cooked and crumbled - 4 oz fresh basil leaves, chopped - 4 oz green onions, chopped

Directions: Pour tomato soup in the pot and preheat on medium heat. Bring to boil. Add vinegar, oregano, butter, turmeric, hot sauce, salt, black pepper, and olive oil. Stir well. Simmer the soup for 5 minutes. Serve soup topped with crumbled bacon, green onion, and basil.

Nutrition: Calories: 397 / Carbs: 9.8g / Fat: 33.8 / Protein: 11.7g

Green Soup

Preparation Time: 12 minutes
Cooking Time: 15 minutes
Servings: 6

Ingredients: 2 cloves garlic - 1 white onion - 1 cauliflower head - 2 oz butter - 1 bay leaf, crushed - 1 cup spinach leaves - ½ cup watercress - 4 cups vegetable stock - Salt and ground black pepper to taste - 1 cup of coconut milk - ½ cup parsley, for serving

Directions: Peel and mince garlic. Peel and dice onion. Divide cauliflower into florets. Preheat pot on medium-high heat, add butter and melt it. Add onion and garlic, stir, and sauté for 4 minutes. Add cauliflower and bay leaf, stir and cook for 5 minutes. Add spinach and watercress, stir and cook for another 3 minutes. Pour in vegetable stock—season with salt and black pepper. Stir and bring to boil. Pour in coconut milk and stir well. Take off heat. Use an immersion blender to blend well. Top with parsley and serve hot.

Nutrition: Calories: 227 / Carbs: 4.89g / Fat: 35.1 / Protein: 6.97g

Sausage and Peppers Soup

Preparation Time: 15 minutes
Cooking Time: 1 hour 15 minutes
Servings: 6

Ingredients:

1 tbsp avocado oil

2 lbs pork sausage meat

Salt and ground black pepper to taste

1 green bell pepper, seeded and chopped

5 oz canned jalapeños, chopped

5 oz canned tomatoes, chopped

1¼ cup spinach - 4 cups beef stock

1 tsp Italian seasoning

1 tbsp cumin - 1 tsp onion powder

1 tsp garlic powder - 1 tbsp chili powder

Directions:

Preheat pot with avocado oil on medium heat. Put sausage meat in pot and brown for 3 minutes on all sides. Add salt, black pepper, and green bell pepper and continue to cook for 3 minutes. Add jalapeños and tomatoes, stir well and cook for 2 minutes more. Toss spinach and stir again close lid and cook for 7 minutes. Pour in beef stock, Italian seasoning, cumin, onion powder, chili powder, garlic powder, salt, and black pepper, stir well. Close lid again. Cook for 30 minutes. When time is up, uncover the pot and simmer for 15 minutes more. Serve hot.

Nutrition:

Calories: 531

Carbohydrates: 3.99g

Fat: 44.5g

Protein: 25.8g

Avocado Soup

Preparation Time: 12 minutes
Cooking Time: 15 minutes
Servings: 4

Ingredients: 2 tbsp butter - 2 scallions, chopped - 3 cups chicken stock - 2 avocados, pitted, peeled, and chopped - Salt and ground black pepper to taste - ⅔ cup heavy cream

Directions: Preheat pot on medium heat, add butter and melt it. Toss scallions, stir, and sauté for 2 minutes. Pour in 2 ½ cups stock and bring to simmer—Cook for 3 minutes. Meanwhile, peel and chop avocados. Place avocado, ½ cup of stock, cream, salt, and pepper in a blender and blend well. Add avocado mixture to the pot and mix well—Cook for 2 minutes. Sprinkle with more salt and pepper, stir. Serve hot.

Nutrition: Calories: 329 / Carbs: 5.9g / Fat: 22.9g / Protein: 5.8g

Roasted Bell Peppers Soup

Preparation Time: 15 minutes
Cooking Time: 20 minutes
Servings: 6

Ingredients: 1 medium white onion - 2 cloves garlic - 2 celery stalks - 12 oz roasted bell peppers, seeded - 2 tbsp olive oil - Salt and ground black pepper to taste - 1-quart chicken stock - 2/3 cup water - ¼ cup Parmesan cheese, grated - ⅔ cup heavy cream

Directions: Peel and chop onion and garlic. Chop celery and bell pepper. Preheat pot with oil on medium heat. Put garlic, onion, celery, salt, and pepper in the pot, stir and sauté for 8 minutes. Pour in chicken stock and water. Add bell peppers and stir. Bring to boil, close lid, and simmer for 5 minutes. Reduce heat if needed. When time is up, blend soup using an immersion blender. Add cream and season with salt and pepper to taste. Take off heat. Serve hot with grated cheese.

Nutrition: Calories: 180 / Carbs: 3.9g / Fat: 12.9g / Protein: 5.9g

Lemon Butter Sauce with Fish

Preparation Time: 10 minutes
Cooking Time: 10 minutes
Servings: 2

Ingredients:

150 g thin white fish fillets - 4 tbsps. butter

2 tbsps. white flour - 2 tbsps. olive oil

1 tbsp. fresh lemon juice - salt and pepper

chopped parsley

Directions: Place the butter in a small skillet over medium heat. Melt it and leave it, just stirring it casually. After 3 mins, pour into a small bowl. Add lemon juice and season it, and set it aside. Dry the fish with paper towels, season it to taste, and sprinkle with flour. Heat oil in a skillet over high heat: when shimmering, add the fish and cook around 2-3 mins. Remove to a plate and serve with the sauce. Top with parsley.

Nutrition: Calories 371 kcal / Fats 27 g / Carbs 3 g / Protein 30 g

Weekend Dinner Stew

Preparation Time: 15 minutes
Cooking Time: 55 minutes
Servings: 6

Ingredients: 1½ lb. grass-fed beef stew meat, trimmed and cubed into 1-inch size - Salt and freshly ground black pepper, to taste - 1 tbsp. olive oil - 1 cup homemade tomato puree - 4 cup homemade beef broth - 2 cup zucchini, chopped - 2 celery ribs, sliced - ½ cup carrots, peeled and sliced - 2 garlic cloves, minced - ½ tbsp. dried thyme 1 tsp. dried parsley - 1 tsp. dried rosemary - 1 tbsp. paprika - 1 tsp. onion powder - 1 tsp. garlic powder

Directions: In a large bowl, add the beef cubes, salt and black pepper and toss to coat well. In a large pan, heat the oil over medium-high heat and cook the beef cubes for about 4-5 minutes or until browned. Add the remaining ingredients and stir to combine. Increase the heat to high and bring to a boil. Reduce the heat to low and simmer, covered for about 40-50 minutes. Stir in the salt and black pepper and remove from the heat. Serve hot.

Nutrition: Calories: 293 / Carbohydrates: 8g / Protein: 9.3g
Fat: 10.7g / Sugar: 4g / Sodium: 223mg / Fiber: 2.3g

Mexican Pork Stew

Preparation Time: 15 minutes
Cooking Time: 2 hours 10 minutes
Servings: 1

Ingredients: 3 tbsp. unsalted butter - 2½ lb. boneless pork ribs, cut into ¾-inch cubes - 1 large yellow onion, chopped - 4 garlic cloves, crushed - 1½ cup homemade chicken broth - 2 (10-oz.) cans sugar-free diced tomatoes - 1 cup canned roasted poblano chiles - 2 tsp. dried oregano - 1 tsp. ground cumin - Salt, to taste - ¼ cup fresh cilantro, chopped - 2 tbsp. fresh lime juice

Directions: In a large pan, melt the butter over medium-high heat and cook the pork, onions and garlic for about 5 minutes or until browned. Add the broth and scrape up the browned bits. Add the tomatoes, poblano chiles, oregano, cumin, and salt and bring to a boil. Reduce the heat to medium-low and simmer, covered for about 2 hours. Stir in the fresh cilantro and lime juice and remove from heat. Serve hot.

Nutrition: Calories: 288 / Carbohydrates: 8.8g / Protein: 39.6g
Fat: 10.1g / Sugar: 4g / Sodium: 283mg / Fiber: 2.8g

Delicious Tomato Basil Soup

Preparation Time: 10 minutes
Cooking Time: 40 minutes
Servings: 4

Ingredients: ¼ cup olive oil - ½ cup heavy cream - 1 lb. tomatoes, fresh - 4 cup chicken broth, divided - 4 cloves garlic, fresh - Sea salt & pepper to taste

Directions: Preheat oven to 400° Fahrenheit and line a baking sheet with foil. Remove the cores from your tomatoes and place them on the baking sheet along with the cloves of garlic. Drizzle tomatoes and garlic with olive oil, salt, and pepper. Roast at 400° Fahrenheit for 30 minutes. Pull the tomatoes out of the oven and place into a blender, along with the juices that have dripped onto the pan during roasting. Add two cups of the chicken broth to the blender. Blend until smooth, then strain the mixture into a large saucepan or a pot. While the pan is on the stove, whisk the remaining two cups of broth and the cream into the soup. Simmer for about ten minutes. Season to taste, then serve hot!

Nutrition: Calories: 225 / Carbs: 5.5 g / Fat: 20 g / Protein: 6.5 g

Hungarian Pork Stew

Preparation Time: 15 minutes
Cooking Time: 2 hours 20 minutes
Servings: 10

Ingredients:

3 tbsp. olive oil - 3½ lb. pork shoulder, cut into 4 portions

1 tbsp. butter - 2 medium onions, chopped

16 oz. tomatoes, crushed - 5 garlic cloves, crushed

2 Hungarian wax peppers, chopped

3 tbsp. Hungarian Sweet paprika - 1 tbsp. smoked paprika

1 tsp. hot paprika - ½ tsp. caraway seeds

1 bay leaf - 1 cup homemade chicken broth

1 packet unflavored gelatin - 2 tbsp. fresh lemon juice

Pinch of xanthan gum

Salt and freshly ground black pepper, to taste

Directions:

In a heavy-bottomed pan, heat 1 tbsp. of oil over high heat and sear the pork for about 2-3 minutes or until browned. Transfer the pork onto a plate and cut into bite-sized pieces. In the same pan, heat 1 tbsp. of oil and butter over medium-low heat and sauté the onions for about 5-6 minutes. With a slotted spoon transfer the onion into a bowl. In the same pan, add the tomatoes and cook for about 3-4 minutes, without stirring. Meanwhile, in a small frying pan, heat the remaining oil over-low heat and sauté the garlic, wax peppers, all kinds of paprika and caraway seeds for about 20-30 seconds. Remove from the heat and set aside. In a small bowl, mix together the gelatin and broth. In the large pan, add the cooked pork, garlic mixture, gelatin mixture and bay leaf and bring to a gentle boil. Reduce the heat to low and simmer, covered for about 2 hours. Stir in the xanthan gum and simmer for about 3-5 minutes. Stir in the lemon juice, salt and black pepper and remove from the heat. Serve hot.

Nutrition:

Calories: 529 / Carbohydrates: 5.8g

Protein: 38.9g / Fat: 38.5g

Sugar: 2.6g / Sodium: 216mg / Fiber: 2.1g

Chicken Enchilada Soup

Preparation Time: 10 minutes
Cooking Time: 45 minutes
Servings: 4

Ingredients:

½ cup fresh cilantro, chopped - 1 ¼ tsp. chili powder

1 cup fresh tomatoes, diced - 1 med. yellow onion, diced

1 small red bell pepper, diced - 1 tbsp. cumin, ground

1 tbsp. extra virgin olive oil - 1 tbsp. lime juice, fresh

1 tsp. dried oregano - 2 cloves garlic, minced

2 lg. stalks celery, diced - 4 cups chicken broth

8 oz. chicken thighs, boneless & skinless, shredded

8 oz. cream cheese, softened

Directions:

In a pot over medium heat, warm olive oil. Once hot, add celery, red pepper, onion, and garlic. Cook for about 3 minutes or until shiny. Stir the tomatoes into the pot and let cook for another 2 minutes. Add seasonings to the pot, stir in chicken broth and bring to a boil. Once boiling, drop the heat down to low and allow to simmer for 20 minutes. Once simmered, add the cream cheese and allow the soup to return to a boil. * Drop the heat once again and allow to simmer for another 20 minutes. Stir the shredded chicken into the soup along with the lime juice and the cilantro. Spoon into bowls and serve hot!

Nutrition:

Calories: 420

Carbohydrates: 9 g

Fat: 29.5 g

Protein: 27 g

DESSERTS

Cottage Cheese Pudding

Preparation Time: 10 minutes
Cooking Time: 45 minutes
Servings: 6

Ingredients: Pudding - 1 cup cottage cheese - ¾ cup heavy cream 3 organic eggs - ¾ cup of water - ½ cups granulated erythritol 1 teaspoon organic vanilla extract - Topping - 1/3 cup heavy whipping cream - 1/3 cup fresh raspberries

Directions: Preheat your oven to 350°F. Grease 6 (6-ounce) ramekins. Add all the ingredients (except cinnamon) and pulse in a blender until smooth. Transfer the mixture into prepared ramekins evenly. Now, place ramekins in a large baking dish. Add hot water in the baking dish, about 1-inch up sides of the ramekins. Bake for about 35 minutes. Serve warm with the topping o heavy whipping cream and raspberries.

Nutrition: Calories: 226 / Fat: 19.6g / Carbs: 3.7g / Protein: 9g

Cream Cake

Preparation Time: 15 minutes
Cooking Time: 1 hour and 5 minutes
Servings: 12

Ingredients:

2 cups almond flour

2 teaspoons organic baking powder

½ cup butter, chopped

2 ounces cream cheese, softened

1 cup sour cream

1 cups granulated erythritol

1 teaspoon organic vanilla extract

4 large organic eggs

1 tablespoon powdered erythritol

Directions:

Preheat your oven to 350°F. Generously, grease a 9-inch Bundt pan. Add almond flour and baking powder in a large bowl and mix well. Set aside. In a microwave-safe bowl, add butter and cream cheese and microwave for about 30 seconds. Remove from microwave and stir well. Add sour cream, erythritol, and vanilla extract and mix until well combined. Add the cream mixture into the bowl of the flour mixture and mix until well combined. Add eggs and mix until well combined. Transfer the mixture into the prepared pan evenly. Bake for about 50 minutes or until a toothpick inserted in the center comes out clean. Remove from the oven and put onto a wire rack to cool for about 10 minutes. Carefully, invert the cake onto a wire rack to cool completely. Just before serving, dust the cake with powdered erythritol. Cut into 12 equal-sized slices and serve.

Nutrition:

Calories: 258

Fat: 24.3g

Carbs: 5.5g

Protein: 7.2g

Keto Shake

Preparation Time: 15 minutes
Cooking Time: 0 minute
Servings: 1

Ingredients: ¾ cup almond milk - ½ cup ice - 2 tablespoons almond butter - 2 tablespoons cocoa powder (unsweetened) 2 tablespoons Swerve - 1 tablespoon chia seeds - 2 tablespoons hemp seeds - ½ tablespoon vanilla extract - Salt to taste

Directions: Blend all the ingredients in a food processor. Chill in the refrigerator before serving.

Nutrition: Calories 104 / Total Fat 9.5g / Saturated Fat 5.1g Cholesterol 0mg / Sodium 24mg / Total Carbohydrate 3.6g / Dietary Fiber 1.4g / Total Sugars 1.1g / Protein 2.9g / Potassium 159mg

Keto Cheesecakes

Preparation Time: 25 minutes
Servings: 9

Ingredients:
For the cheesecakes: 2 tablespoons butter - 1 tablespoon caramel syrup; sugar-free   3 tablespoons coffee - 8 ounces cream cheese 1/3 cup swerve - 3 eggs
For the frosting: 8 ounces mascarpone cheese; soft - 3 tablespoons caramel syrup; sugar-free / 2 tablespoons swerve - 3 tablespoons butter

Directions: In your blender, mix cream cheese with eggs, 2 tablespoons butter, coffee, 1 tablespoon caramel syrup, and 1/3 cup swerve and pulse very well. Spoon this into a cupcakes pan, introduce in the oven at 350 degrees F and bake for 15 minutes. Leave aside to cool down and then keep in the freezer for 3 hours. Meanwhile, in a bowl, mix 3 tablespoons butter with 3 tablespoons caramel syrup, 2 tablespoons swerve, and mascarpone cheese and blend well. Spoon this over cheesecakes and serve them.

Nutrition: Calories: 478.2 / Total Fat: 47.8 g / Cholesterol: 140.4 mg / Sodium: 270.7 mg/ Potassium: 233.7 mg / Total Carbohydrate: 9.4 g / Protein: 9.2 g

Keto Brownies

Preparation Time: 30 minutes
Servings: 12

Ingredients: 6 ounces coconut oil; melted - 4 ounces cream cheese - 5 tablespoons swerve - 6 eggs - 2 teaspoons vanilla - 3 ounces of cocoa powder - 1/2 teaspoon baking powder

Directions: In a blender, mix eggs with coconut oil, cocoa powder, baking powder, vanilla, cream cheese, and swerve and stir using a mixer. Pour this into a lined baking dish, introduce in the oven at 350 degrees F and bake for 20 minutes. Slice into rectangle pieces when their cold and serve

Nutrition: Calories: 183.7 / Total Fat: 16.6 g / Cholesterol: 20.7 mg Sodium: 36.3 mg/ Potassium: 21.6 mg / Total Carbohydrate: 4.9 g Protein: 1.4 g

Raspberry and Coconut

Preparation Time: 15 minutes
Servings: 12

Ingredients: 1/4 cup swerve - 1/2 cup coconut oil - 1/2 cup raspberries; dried - 1/2 cup coconut; shredded - 1/2 cup coconut butter

Directions: In your food processor, blend dried berries very well. Heat a pan with the butter over medium heat. Add oil, coconut and swerve; stir and cook for 5 minutes. Pour half of this into a lined baking pan and spread well. Add raspberry powder and also spread. Top with the rest of the butter mix, spread and keep in the fridge for a while Cut into pieces and serve

Nutrition: Carbohydrates: 45g / Sugar: 30g / Fat: 42g / Protein: 8g / Cholesterol: 0mg

Chocolate Pudding Delight

Preparation Time: 52 minutes
Servings: 2

Ingredients: 1/2 teaspoon stevia powder - 2 tablespoons cocoa powder - 2 tablespoons water - 1 tablespoon gelatin - 1 cup of coconut milk - 2 tablespoons maple syrup

Directions: Heat a pan with the coconut milk over medium heat; add stevia and cocoa powder and stir well. In a bowl, mix gelatin with water; stir well and add to the pan. Stir well, add maple syrup, whisk again, divide into ramekins and keep in the fridge for 45 minutes Serve cold.

Nutrition: Calories: 221.2/ Total Fat: 13.6 g / Cholesterol: 9.8 mg / Sodium: 250.3 mg / Potassium: 86.7 mg / Total Carbohydrate: 22.7 g / Protein: 3.4 g

Peanut Butter Fudge

Preparation Time: 2 hours 12 minutes
Servings: 12

Ingredients: 1 cup peanut butter; unsweetened - 1 cup of coconut oil - 1/4 cup almond milk - 2 teaspoons vanilla stevia - A pinch of salt

For the topping: 2 tablespoons swerve - 1/4 cup cocoa powder 2 tablespoons melted coconut oil

Directions: In a heatproof bowl, mix peanut butter with 1 cup coconut oil; stir and heat up in your microwave until it melts. Add a pinch of salt, almond milk, and stevia; stir well everything and pour into a lined loaf pan. Keep in the fridge for 2 hours and then slice it. In a bowl, mix 2 tablespoons melted coconut with cocoa powder and swerve and stir very well. Drizzle the sauce over your peanut butter fudge and serve

Nutrition: Calories 85 /Fat 4.7g / Saturated Fat 2.7g / Protein 0.5g

Cinnamon Streusel Egg Loaf

Preparation Time: 10 minutes

Cooking Time: 15 minutes

Servings: 2

Ingredients:

2 tbsp almond flour

1 tbsp butter, softened

½ tbsp grated butter, chilled

1 egg / 1-ounce cream cheese

Others: ½ tsp cinnamon, divided

1 tbsp erythritol sweetener, divided

¼ tsp vanilla extract, unsweetened

Directions:

Turn on the oven, then set it to 350 degrees F and let it preheat. Meanwhile, crack the egg in a small bowl, add cream cheese, softened butter, ¼ tsp cinnamon, ½ tbsp sweetener, and vanilla and whisk until well combined. Divide the egg batter between two silicone muffins and then bake for 7 minutes. Meanwhile, prepare the streusel and for this, place flour in a small bowl, add remaining ingredients and stir until well mixed. When egg loaves have baked, sprinkle streusel on top and then continue baking for 7 minutes. When done, remove loaves from the cups, let them cool for 5 minutes and then

Nutrition:

Calories 15

Fats 14.8 g

Protein 4 g

Carbs 1.3 g

Fiber 1 g

Snickerdoodle Muffins

Preparation Time: 10 minutes
Cooking Time: 12 minutes
Servings: 2

Ingredients: 6 2/3 tbsp coconut flour - ½ of egg - 1 tbsp butter, unsalted, melted - 1 1/3 tbsp whipping cream - 1 tbsp almond milk, unsweetened - Others: 1 1/3 tbsp erythritol sweetener and more for topping - ¼ tsp baking powder - ¼ tsp ground cinnamon and more for topping - ¼ tsp vanilla extract, unsweetened

Directions: Turn on the oven, then set it to 350 degrees F and let it preheat. Meanwhile, take medium bowl, place flour in it, add cinnamon, baking powder, and cinnamon and stir until combined. Take a separate bowl, place the half egg in it, add butter, sour cream, milk, and vanilla and whisk until blended. Whisk in flour mixture into incorporated and smooth batter comes together, divide the batter evenly between two silicon muffin cups and then sprinkle cinnamon and sweetener on top. Bake the muffins for 10 to 12 minutes until firm, and then the top has turned golden brown and then Serve and enjoy!

Nutrition: Calories: 241 / Fats: 21 g / Protein: 7 g / Net Carbs: 3 g / Fiber: 3 g

Yogurt and Strawberry Bowl

Preparation Time: 5 minutes
Cooking Time: 0 minutes
Servings: 2

Ingredients:

3 oz mixed berries

1 tbsp chopped almonds

1 tbsp chopped walnuts

4 oz yogurt

Directions: Divide yogurt between two bowls, top with berries, and then sprinkle with almonds and walnuts. Serve and enjoy!

Nutrition:

Calories: 165

Fats: 11.2 g

Protein: 9.3 g

Net Carbohydrates: 2.5 g

Fiber: 1.8 g

Sweet Cinnamon Muffin

Preparation Time: 5 minutes
Cooking time: 2 minutes
Servings: 2

Ingredients:

4 tsp coconut flour

2 tsp cinnamon

2 tsp erythritol sweetener

1/16 tsp baking soda - 2 eggs

Directions: Take a medium bowl, place all the ingredients in it, and whisk until well combined. Take two ramekins, grease them with oil, distribute the prepared batter in it and then microwave for 1 minute and 45 seconds until done. When done, take out muffin from the ramekin, cut in half, and then. Serve and enjoy!

Nutrition: Calories: 101 / Fats: 6.5 g / Protein: 7.6 g / Carbs: 0.5 g / Fiber: 1.7 g

Nutty Muffins

Preparation Time: 5 minutes
Cooking Time: 5 minutes
Servings: 2

Ingredients:

4 tsp coconut flour

1/16 tsp baking soda

1 tsp erythritol sweetener

2 eggs - 2 tsp almond butter, unsalted

Directions: Take a medium bowl, place all the ingredients in it, and whisk until well combined. Take two ramekins, grease them with oil, distribute the prepared batter in it and then microwave for 1 minute and 45 seconds until done. When done, take out muffin from the ramekin, cut in half, and then Serve and enjoy!

Nutrition: Calories: 131 / Fats: 8.6 g / Protein: 8.4 g / Carbs: 2.3 g / Fiber: 2.2 g

CONCLUSION

As women grow older, there are a variety of changes occurring within their bodies. Having a great deal of impact, estrogen reduction often causes weight gain and a slower metabolism. The keto diet, with adjustments for the particular requirements of women over fifty years old, is a beautiful way to lose weight while relieving some of the aches and pains experienced as the lack of estrogen takes hold. By adapting the diet to make it more palatable for women over the age of 50, the ketogenic diet can be beneficial in more ways than just weight loss. Follow the principles of food choices suggested by studies performed around the world and reap the benefits of this popular diet. Ease into ketosis with the plan outlined, and you will find a smoother transition to a low-carbohydrate lifestyle. Use the tips and tricks to smooth over rough spots and use the food list to try new foods.

While on the Keto diet, you are building up energy stores for your body to utilize. This means that you should be feeling a necessary boost in your energy levels and the ability to get through each moment of each day without struggling. You can say goodbye to the sluggish feeling that often accompanies other diet plans. When you are on Keto, you should only be experiencing the benefits of additional energy and unlimited potential. Your diet isn't going to always feel like a diet. After some time, you will realize that you enjoy eating a Keto menu very much. Because your body will be switching the way it metabolizes, it will also be switching what it craves. Don't be surprised if you end up craving fats and proteins as you progress on the Keto diet — this is what your body will eventually want. Keto diet helps control blood sugar and improve nutrition, which in turn not only improves insulin response and resistance but also protects against memory loss, which is often a part of aging.

You have the tools to reach success in losing weight on the keto diet. In the end, the weight loss will be a very generous reward you will enjoy. Thank you once again!